Loving
Through
Heartsongs

Written and Illustrated by
Mattie J.T. Stepanek
Poet & Peacemaker

Foreword by Maya Angelou

VSP Books
HYPERION
NEW YORK

Library of Congress Cataloging-in-Publication Data

Stepanek, Mattie J.T. (Mattie Joseph Thaddeus)
Loving through heartsongs / Mattie J. T. Stepanek—1st ed.
p. cm.
ISBN 0-7868-6946-1
1. Muscular dystrophy in children—Patients—Poetry. I. Title.

PS3619.T4765 L68 2003   2002032865
813'.54—dc21

Hyperion books are available for special promotions and premiums.
For details contact Hyperion Special Markets, 77 West 66th Street, 11th floor,
New York, New York 10023, or call 212-456-0133.

First Edition
10 9 8 7 6 5 4 3 2 1

This book is dedicated to my friend Oprah Winfrey.
You are a true humanitarian who touches minds and hearts
and spirits around the world with gifts of love and life.
"I love you and you love me."

—Love always, from "your guy," Mattie

Acknowledgments

Welcome to the fifth and final book in the original Heartsongs series, *Loving Through Heartsongs*. My hope is that I will have the opportunity to publish more books that include my poetry and essays and thoughts on life. Until then, I would like to acknowledge some very important people and groups that have helped me "love living" and "celebrate" and "hope" through my "journey" and "heartsongs."

Thank you to Peter and Cheryl Barnes and to Bob Miller for providing me with the first doors for sharing my messages of hope and peace through my poetry. Thank you to Oprah Winfrey, *Good Morning America*, Larry King, Chris Cuomo, Brian O'Keefe, Michael Watts, and Paula Zahn for repeatedly opening the doors for me so that I can share with so many people around the world. And thank you to Kelly Ellison and The Children's Peace Pavilion in Independence, Missouri, and to Shelly Sackstein and Action Long Island, New York, for welcoming me as I stepped through the doors, and allowing me to share my thoughts with so many children.

Thank you to Maya Angelou, Jerry Lewis, Gary Zukav, and Jimmy Carter for taking the time to share their thoughts about my messages by writing the forewords to my books. And a thank you to all the people who have written such beautiful and inspirational notes to me...I open and read and appreciate every letter, and wish that it were possible for me to personally respond to every single person.

Thank you to Ron Hemelgarn, Jeff Bouchard, Christopher Cross, Vito D'Anna, Jann Carl, and their families for inviting my mom and me to share with them as they celebrate their love for life. Thank you to Ride-Away Accessible Transportation (especially Paul, Kurt, Fred, and Bryant of Clinton, Maryland) for keeping my mom and me safely on the road in our Sophie-van so I can share my messages with people all over America, and to the mystery benefactor who provided me with a new Invacare wheelchair through Mid-Atlantic Healthcare. And thank you to the Marriott Corporation (especially Gerry Keyes in Chicago, Illinois, and Pam Follette in Gaithersburg, Maryland) for giving us a place to stay when things were tight.

Thank you to Sue Hendrickson, Stacy Han, and Canine Companions for Independence for Micah Brackenhollow Stepanek—my beautiful golden retriever puppy and best friend in the world. Thank you to Children's National Medical Center in Washington, D.C., and to Children's Hospice International for my life, my spirit, and my dreams. And a very special thank you to Tim O'Brien for providing so much pro bono legal support for me so that my book venture is secure, to Leslie Billman for making sure my interests and future are secure, and to Bob Barnett and Denean Howell for securing the contract with Hyperion for me.

Thank you to the Muscular Dystrophy Association, especially Mike Blishak, Jerry Lewis, Bob Ross, Gerry Weinberg, Chris Medvesic, Tom Boyle, Katie McGuire, Annie Kennedy, Gina Clarke, Cathy and John Toth, Stephanie Goldklang, Melissa Mays, DJ and Tom O'Connor, and Ann Simmons, and to supporters of MDA like Harold Schaitberger, Ron Kuley, the IAFF, Harley Davidson, CITGO, 7-Up, MARS Supermarkets, Roger Claxton, Randy Cisulak, Bubba-Bert Mentrassi, J. J. Jackson, Kevin Reilly, and all the others... you are a true celebration of hope and love.

Thank you to my friends and teachers and counselors and doctors and heroes—especially Jimmy Carter, the Newcombs and Dobbinses, the Beaudets, the Retzlaffs and Odens, the Moxes, the Wyatts, the Holy Rosary Family, the Pauls, the Gagnes, the Stacks and Crismans, the Trescas, Devin Dressman, Andi Slavic, Valerie Etherton, Terry Spearman, Peggy Stypula, Mollie Thorn, Candie Schwartz, Michael Lancaster, Libby Moore and Shelley Heesacker (Harpo), Jeanne Meyers (myhero.com), Alan Johnson (Atlanta RW Goodtimes), Martin Doblemeier (Journey Films), Nile Rogers (We Are Family), Judy Verses (Verizon), Mark Barondess, Mary Hogarth (Toys "R" Us), Mary Ellen O'Neill and Camille McDuffie (Hyperion), Jim Hawkins, Mary Paul, Laura Becker, Kim Fenton, Kim Witzmann, Bob Fink, Christie Corriveaux, Marissa Garris, Russ Yates (Holiday Park and "Mattie's Landing"), Grandmaster Yong Sung Lee, and Master Dong Kim... you have given so many chances to learn and grow and be, and I love you so much for everything. A special kinship thank you to Mary Lou, Jo Ann, and all the members of the immediate and extended Smith family (especially Melvin, who showed me his teeth under the table!), for being there for my mom and me, and for helping us play after every storm.

Thank you to all of the children I have known who died so early in mortal years—like my siblings, Katie, Stevie, and Jamie, and my friends and PICU roommates like Danny, Rebecca, John, A.J., Christian, Alyssa, Daniel, and so many others with known spirits but not known names...I believe that each of you is still loving the eternal gift of Life, and that you are loving each of us as we grow closer to the reality of Loving Through Heartsongs. Through creation and God, by whatever name, you are the root of my inspiration.

And to my mom...thank you for love and lessons and life. You have helped me become a poet, a peacemaker, and a philosopher who plays, and the best person that I can be. You have been, and always will be, my hero.

—Love, Mattie J.T. Stepanek

Foreword

The poet may not be able to interpret the words written on the wall, but he does see the wall and his response may be a proclamation or an alarm, because many people do not see the wall. Mattie Stepanek not only sees the wall, but he has counted every plank and knows intimately what lives behind the wall.

In his poem "Post-Terrorism Haiku" (from *Celebrate Through Heartsongs*), he reminds us that we are the land of the free, not of the vengeful, and that it is in God we trust, not in bombs and guns.

It is remarkable that a person so young could have the wisdom to write, "It matters that the world knows we must celebrate the gift of life every day. We must remember to play after every storm."

Mattie J.T. Stepanek means to lift up every person, lift up every human being and carry us all across the finish line, each of us first, each of us a winner. Thank you, Mattie!

Maya Angelou

Contents

Finding Love from Lessons

Unfolding

Born of the
Dust of humility,
Spread on the
Wings of pride,
Carried by
Winds of hope,
I grow with the
Ebbing life tide.

January 2001

Learning Nothing?

It's impossible
To learn nothing.
Even when you believe
You are learning nothing,
You are actually
Still learning something.
Consider each day, each moment,
Each possible lesson, carefully.
Some place thought to be
Not of interest turns
Out to be wonderful.
Some time with a friend
Just chatting and sharing
Becomes a treasured memory.
Some thing almost unnoticed
Prompts a realization
Towards a philosophy for life.
It is truly impossible
To learn nothing
When you believe.

June 2002

Gift-Rapt

Share the gift of courage,
And it may lead to forgiveness.
Share the gift of forgiveness,
And it may lead to hope.
Share the gift of hope,
And it may lead to peace.
This year, and every day,
Let us share gifts of the heart,
Which grow from a belief in
Something greater than us—
That which was before us,
That which is with us,
That which will be beyond us.
Let us think gently,
Speak gently,
Live gently...
And the world may be
Blessed gently
With the greatest gift of all...
Faith.

December 2001

On Being Rich

I used to think
That being rich
Meant...
Having lots and
LOTS of money,
And getting
And doing
Everything
You want.
But I was wrong.
Now I know
That being rich
Means...
Having lots and
LOTS of love,
Honesty,
Respect,
And friends.
So no matter
How poor
Or wealthy
You may be,
It is always
Friends and
Gifts of the heart
That really count.

July 1999

Heaven's Smile

On New Year's Eve, look out at the moon
That will bring new tomorrows.
And if the moon is God's thumb-nail,
Then you can see Heaven's smile.
Know that the smile is a gift,
In the middle of the Angel-Stars
Watching over us from above.
Know that the cold air of winter brings us hugs,
As we keep tightly with each other for warmth.
If you understand this,
It will help you to get wiser and stronger.
It will help our Heartsongs to grow.
It will help peace to spread in the world.
It will help Mother Earth to live another year.
And if you see a shooting star,
Know that it is very special
Even if we don't really get to wish on it.
Understand that the gift is to our heart, and
We can always wish within our heart.
My wish, even if it is only in my heart,
Is for a safer next year that is not so rough,
And that I am wishing on the eve of
A peaceful new year, and years.
So remember,
Every New Year's Eve, look up into the sky, and
See Heaven's smile in whatever moon is there.
It will be a reflection of life and love,
And a gift for you to meditate
About the past, the present, and our future,
As we get stronger in understanding each year.

December 1997

About Dunderheads

When laughing with,
Everyone has fun
Playing the fool.
When laughing at,
The teaser is a
Lone, sad
Kind of fool.

October 2000

A Taming Lesson

The Little Prince had
A very kind, gentle,
Poetic-living mind...
And that
Is what all people
Of the world need.

December 1998

Flowing Thoughtfulness

When one person
Is thoughtful to another,
The thoughtfulness
Gets carried on and on.
It is like a river of kindness,
Once blocked by rocks,
That is suddenly opened
By a single person's
Kind thought or act.
The river runs freely again,
And continues to flow,
Moving more rocks and
Reaching the hearts of others.
When one person
Is thoughtful to another
The thoughtfulness
Gets carried on and on.
The more we get together
And help each other,
The more friendship
There can be throughout
Many different places.

The friendship can begin
Like a small stream
In a single neighborhood,
And then expand throughout
A river of districts, states,
Countries, and even continents.
When one person
Is thoughtful to another,
The thoughtfulness
Gets carried on and on.
Soon, we could have
A whole ocean of friendships,
And that's how
The world was created,
And how
It should always be.

May 2000

9

About Promises

Promises
Should be
Taken seriously
Because
They involve
Something
That will
Somehow
Touch
The future
Of some life.

April 2000

Royal Decree

Once you make a friend,
Never stop being a friend to them.
Celebrate all the holidays, somehow.
Don't drink alcohol unwisely.
Do not be evil, mean, or bad.
Don't say any bad words,
Especially words like "Shut Up!"
Believe in the Clean-Dish Fairy.
Put on the porch light if
A family member is out after dark.
Use your best manners, no exceptions.
Always have an interest.
Be gentle with people and the earth.
Don't do any bad things.
Be patient with yourself and others.
Be good everywhere you are and go.
Decree that you love life, every day.

April 1998

11

To Langston Hughes

Bold adventures of daring events,
Exciting discoveries to share,
Creating a fun world in each of our minds,
To hold and remember each night.
Plans for the future, thoughts of the past,
Thinking with freedom, yet care,
If only the whole world could hold fast to dreams,
Perhaps we'd find peace in plain sight.

February 2000

Witnessing
Love
in Creation

Rapture

Have you witnessed
The early morning?
Right before the
Sun rises, and
The sky glows
Purple lava-lamp?
The clouds are
The dark,
Floating
Lumps, and
The still
Gentle earth
Is to look upon.

December 2000

Deer Watching

Quiet, calm, peaceful,
Solemn-eyed, but alert.
These are the deer,
Prancing through the
Forest to the meadow.
Quiet, calm, peaceful,
Solemn-eyed, but alert.
These are the people
Who notice the deer,
Prancing through the
Forest to the meadow.

August 1998

Winter Magic

The winter snow flurries,
The soft, furry flurries,
Look like fireflies.
Winter fireflies that glow in the light.
Like summer fireflies
Light up a summer night,
The shiny, glittery snow fireflies
Light up a winter night.
I look at them and I think,
"I can't wait for spring,
and then summer,
and then fireflies and butterflies."
In the summer,
I like to watch the fireflies
In the warm outdoors.
In the winter,
I like to watch the magical ones,
Or sometimes,
I catch them on my
Tongue, or hand, or finger,
And make wishes.

February 1996

18

Spring-Kinging

Today is the first day of spring!
The air will get warmer and warmer.
The flowers will begin to
Peek out from under the ground.
And I, the Snow-King, will soon
Melt down into the earth, then
Rise up again as the Spring-King!
As the Snow-King,
I calmed the winds and
Fought the Snow-Villains.
As the Spring-King,
I will make blossoms grow
On the winter-stick trees
That live behind our house.
The blossoms will be like lace
And then change into leaves.
I will make the brown-scratchy
Grass turn soft and green.
I will make rainbow-flowers
That invite butterflies and bees
To drink their juice and take seeds
Away with them to make baby-flowers.
I will be a good Spring-King
For the whole season, until
It's time to grow and change again.

March 1996

Lucky Day

I like the water-rain.
And mommies do.
And teachers do.
And Mother Gooses, too.
The flowers drink it.
The plants drink it.
And this is your lucky day—
You can drink it, too.

August 1993

20

Sticking Around

Today is only the second
Day of summer, and already
I am a Humid-Being.
My clothes are sticking to me,
And I am sticking to my clothes,
And my clothes and I are both
Sticking to the seats and grass,
And just about everything is sticking
To everything else, because the
Summer season is finally here again.
Well, I guess I better be
Sticking a popsicle in my mouth
And then sticking myself into a pool.
Aaaaahhhhhh...
Summer's sticking around for a few months,
And that's okay!

June 1997

21

The Season Tree

I have a special tree
Called the Season Tree.
The Season Tree has
The normal parts
Of a normal tree—
A trunk, and roots.
But, this tree has special branches.
One part of this tree has limbs flowing
With soft, pink snow blossoms
And nests of the first birds
Returning from their journey
To avoid the bitter cold
And scarce food of winter.
These are the spring branches
Of the Season Tree.
Another part of this tree is crowned
With a legion of bright green leaves,
A bounty of the nests for various birds,
And space for the hives of honeybees.
These are the summer branches
Of the Season Tree.
Another part of this tree is smothered
In the cries of migrating birds,
Moving in order
To avoid the struggles of winter.
Flowered with a rainbow of jewel leaves,
Burrowing animals witness them falling
Gently to the ground, swaying
Back and forth, back and forth,
Like hypnotizing cobras.
These are the autumn branches of the Season Tree.

Another part of this tree is bathed
In cold snow clouds,
Drooping with the weight
Of sharp arctic blasts, looking as if
It was wearing undyed
Wool sweaters to keep warm.
These are the winter branches
Of the Season Tree.
But the laden sticks will drop
The cold coverings, to melt into
The warming ground below,
The first signs of a new year dawning
Through the Season Tree,
Which will soon be blessed again,
With the soft, pink blanket of blossoms.
This tree symbolizes the cycle of life.
It reminds us that eventually,
Everything will die,
Into a new Life.
I have a special tree
Called the Season Tree.
The Season Tree has
Many lessons in its branches,
About life and the future,
Which grows from the past.
Each cycle of seasons,
Like those witnessed
Of the Season Tree,
Inspires me to live on,
And on, and on, and on,
Until my time comes
To be a part of the eternal future.

April 2000

Metaphor Lesson (XIII)

At night, the moon is
The marble eye of a
Curious rabbit, looking
Upon the world with interest.

April 2000

24

Sharing
Love Through
People

For Males: About Mating

When a boy penguin wants a female,
He gives her a shiny and special pebble.
When a boy squirrel wants a female,
He gives her a whole bunch of crunchy nuts.
When a boy bear wants a female,
He gives her a huge pile of the juiciest berries.
But, when a boy human wants a female,
He should give her the gifts of respect and love...
Or he shouldn't have a female and marry at all.

April 1997

27

About Friendship

It is good to have a friend...
Someone to comfort, and
Someone to be comforted by.
Someone to trust, and
Someone to be trusted by.
Someone to play with, and
Someone who will play with you.
It is good to have a friend...
A true friend offers respect and honesty.
A true friend shows consideration and trust.
A true friend cares and supports gently.
True friends work together as a team.
It is good to have a friend...
Friendship is a very special gift.
Friendship is a very special bond.
Friendship is a very special relationship
Between and among people.
It is good to have a friend...
When one has a friend,
One can feel loved for being oneself.
When one has a friend,
One can believe and rejoice in the moment.
When one has a friend,
One can travel through life in contentment.
It is good to have a friend...
Hand-to-hand,
Heart-to-heart,
Spirit-to-spirit,
Friendship is the key that opens
The door to harmony,
The river of peace, and
The hope of the future.
It is good to have, and to be, a friend.

August 2000

My LADYBUG

Laura is my ladybug,
Always magical and special,
Dances to midnight organ music.
Yo-yos aren't as fun as my Laura.
Beautiful as the beach sunset,
Usually with a smile on her face.
Gift from the north is my
    Ladybug Laura.

July 1998

Annie Butterfly

Annie, Annie, Butterfly,
Flutter there, flutter by,
Annie, Annie, Butterfly,
Hair as gold as summer skies,
Pretty as the butterflies.

July 1998

29

First Anniversary Prayer

Dear God,
When Lauren moved away,
My Heartsong felt so sad that
It crumbled into little pieces.
And Now, I am so Sad.
But even though my heart is broken,
I still have all the pieces inside, and
I can put them back together again.
It's like when my brother, Jamie, died.
I will always be able to see
Where the breaks were, but
I can have my Heartsong altogether again.
It's sad to have a broken heart.
But, I think it's even sadder for people
Who have never had a broken heart.
If your heart is hard and cold like stone
And the toughest materials of the universe,
It can't break, and you don't hurt.
But if your heart has never broken,
It means you've never had a heart
Soft and warm enough to
Really love someone else.
I will put the pieces of my heart together.
I will always love Lauren, and
I will miss her until she comes back. And,
I will know that my Heartsong has
A good spirit, because it can break.
Thank you, God,
For the gift of a soft heart,
And for all the pieces of my Heartsong.
Amen.

October 1997

30

The First Step

How many thousands of miles
Away from me
Lives my childhood wife?
She is on the Pacific Ocean,
I am on the Atlantic Ocean.
We are a whole country apart,
But we will be together again,
Sometime,
In some year.
And even though we are
So very, very far apart,
We will stay married to each other.
I will be friends with other girls, and
She will be friends with other boys.
That is important for children.
But I just hope that she is not
Picking up a shoe with another boy.
Picking up a shoe
Is the very first step
In "tying the knot" you know.

March 1998

Build a Poem (I)

Valerie...
Valerie is a welcome mat.
She is like an open door.
'She listens, supports, encourages.
She's my social worker...
Valerie.

Build a Poem (II)

Hope...
Hope is a flower.
She is like a spreading rainbow.
She radiates, cares, and plays.
She's my best friend...
Hope.

Build a Poem (III)

Nick...
Nick is a thinker.
He is like a puzzle being put
  together.
He plans, creates, and succeeds.
He's my big kin-brother...
Nick.

Build a Poem (IV)

Ben...
Ben is a sports maniac.
He is like an invincible, rolling
  wheel.
He runs, rides, and really rocks.
He's my younger kin-brother...
Ben.

May 2000

For Mrs. Diane

I'd write you a poem
About a beautiful house,
But never about a furry brown—
  Hmmm...
I'd write you a poem
About a lovely straw hat,
But never about an ugly gray—
  Hmmm...
I'd write you a poem
About a mountain lake,
But never about a slithering—
  Hmmm...
I'd write you a poem
About a kiss and a hug,
But never about a crawling—
  Hmmm...
I love you so much,
That's so very true,
That I'd never use
These words in a poem for you:
  MOUSE!
  RAT!
  SNAKE!
  BUG!

July 1998

34

The Granny Poem

Violets are blue,
And roses are red.
You have the hives,
So please stay in bed.

Sunset is orange,
Bright skies are blue.
Please get well soon,
'Cause I really love you.

July 1998

Children Live What They Learn

When I was a little baby,
I didn't have toys in the bathtub,
And I didn't know how to talk.
You held me and
Rocked me and
Tickled me under my chin.
You loved me so much and
You talked to me.
And then,
When I grew
Into a big little boy,
I played with toys in the tub,
And I knew how to talk
And how to be gentle and caring.
So now,
I can say
I love you, too, Mommy.

December 1993

The Sonnet

Marie, Marie,
Jewel of the sea,
Velvet brown hair,
Eyes that match perfectly.
Marie, Marie,
Jewel of the sea,
Fair and gentle
As any could be.
Marie, Marie,
Jewel of the sea,
Heart as kind
As one can see.
Marie, Marie,
Jewel of the sea.

July 2001

Anniversary Thought

Just a little while ago,
A day, a year, or more ago,
My hand and yours were clasped in love.
In death now, my heart is a treasure box of memories...
Eternally, our spirits are bonded in brotherhood.

November 1999

38

Choice Vows

In the beginning,
Love
Was created,
And it was good.
Yet, as it is
With all things,
Love is a choice.
In the now,
A bond
Is created,
And it is good.
Yet, as it is
With all things,
A bond
Is a choice.
In each tomorrow,
The future
Will be created,
And it can be good.
Yet, as it is
With all things,
The future
Is a choice.

As the love of yesterday
Binds the present into a touch
Towards every tomorrow,
Do not vow
To renew your choices
On your first, your fifth,
Or your fiftieth anniversary.
Rather,
From this moment,
Go forth vowing.
Go forth
Vowing to choose gently,
Celebrating life each day.
Go forth
Vowing to choose wisely,
Playing after every storm.
Go forth
Vowing to choose fervently,
Never giving up hope
In things that matter.
Then, as it was in the beginning,
And, as it is now,
Yet, it will be in the future...
Blessed with choices, and good.

June 2002

39

A Perfect Fit

God created everything, and
God created everyone.
God created all the birds,
And all the fish, and all the plants.
God created all the animals, and
God created all the people.
And, God made something
Very, very special inside the people—
It's in the middle of the people,
But a little to the left—
And it's called a "heart."
Hearts come in red and pink and gold
And black and brown and white.
Hearts come in all these colors
And all the colors in between.
Some of them are my favorite colors,
And that is as special as a heart.
A heart is special because
It is where we feel and love.
A heart is where our body and our spirit
Touch while we are alive.
The more we love,
The bigger our heart gets.
But God made sure that
No matter how big our heart gets from love,
It still fits perfectly, right where it is,
Inside all of the people.

January 1996

40

Keeping
Love Amid
Challenges

Making Wishes

The best time to make a wish is when
You throw a penny in the fountain.
The best time to make a wish is when
You see the first star.
The best time to make a wish is when
You blow out the candles on your cake.
And the very best time to make a wish is when
You have a special prayer in your heart.

March 1998

43

Pinocchio Thoughts

Sometimes,
Fairies come from Heaven,
And turn boys who died
Back into real live boys.
And sometimes,
Fairies don't come,
And boys who died
Can't come back.

November 1993

The Interpreter

Sometimes,
My mommy says,
"Good Heavens!"
I know why she says that.
It is because Jamie is there.
If Jamie came back to us,
We would be so happy—
But then,
My mommy would have to say,
"Sad Heavens."

June 1994

44

Touch of Love

Matties like to touch
Pumpkins and toys.
So, Matties touch them.
Matties don't like to touch
Yucky things and fire.
So, Matties don't touch them.
But Matties can't touch
Jamies anymore,
Even if they want to.
So Matties touch their tears instead.

October 1993

Resignation...Without Resolution

Once there were two little boys,
And their names were Jesus.
They were both the same.
One day, Jesus got sick,
So they went to see the doctor.
The doctor gave them a checkup,
Looked in their eyes, ears, mouth, and trach,
And listened to them with a stethoscope.
Then Jesus had to get an x-ray
On a table that moved all around.
It was very scary.
The doctor also took a picture
Of their heart, through their bellies.
After awhile,
Jesus got to go home from the hospital.
Jesus went home and looked in the mirror,
And saw that they were happy and proud.
"We were very brave," they said.
Then, they went to bed.
One night, one Jesus died,
But the other one woke up in the morning.
He went and looked into the mirror,
And saw that he was sad and alone.
He covered his face
Because he didn't want anyone to see
The tears coming out of his eyes.
Later, they went to church.
One of the Jesuses got buried,
But the other prayed.
He prayed to all of the children,
Because sometimes children die,
And sometimes they don't die.
They just cry, and cry, and cry.

47

November 1993

In Search of Wings

WITCH: Now walk!

BOY: But I don't have any ruby slippers!

WITCH: I know that.

BOY: And I don't have any wings!

WITCH: I know that.
You have to "ching" if you want wings!

BOY: But I don't know how to ching.
I am not magic.

WITCH: Then you have to die to get wings.
If you aren't magic,
To get wings, you have to die.

BOY: But I don't want to die.

WITCH: Then you can't walk with the Big Kids,
Because you fall too easy.
And you can't fly with the Angels,
Because you don't have any wings.

BOY: Oh, I am so sad!
Please ching me, Witch.
Please ching me some wings.

WITCH: No. Sorry. I can't.
You see,
Magic is For-Never.
And wings are For-Ever.

October 1994

48

Parking Lot Omen

Great foreboding moth.
Green of beauty.
Green of mortality.
Green of fervent,
Yet futile effort.
Fluttering
Forward.
To Nowhere.
Or perhaps,
Probably,
The Forever
Of death.
Filling my mind.
With thoughts
Of death.
Fumbling,
I whisper.
Confiding
My fear.

Hello moth.
And then,
Soon, in
Some when,
Goodbye.
Something looming.
In my mind.
In the air.
In the sense
Of death.
Where the
Green of life
Flutters,
Forever,
Into forsaking
Emptiness.

June 2002

49

Stubbling Sadness

If my mommy died,
I would be so sad.
I would lock myself in my room
For a Very Long time,
And not talk to anyone.
Then,
I would come out,
Get over it,
And learn to shave off
All the stubble I grew.

November 2001

50

About Death

Isn't it odd
That such a short word
Means something so eternal?
Isn't it ironic
That such a morbid word
Rhymes with life-giving breath?
Isn't it tragic
That such a real, final word
Touches children, our future, each day?
Isn't it sombering
That such a grown-up, dreaded word
Plays with my memories, my thoughts, my life?

July 2001

51

Psalm of Tad 358

Lord, You have
Saved me from sadness,
And lifted me to light.
  All my life,
  I have been haunted
  By the darkness,
  Only my dreams gave me sight.
  But my Savior
  Has now turned me
  Back to light,
  No longer do I dwell in shadows.
Lord, You have
Saved me from sadness,
And lifted me to light.
  Lord, You comfort me
  In Your gentle arms,
  You dry tears
  Of sadness from my eyes.
  My God,
  I forever await You in hope,
  From the ashes of Job
  I arise.

Lord, You have
Saved me from sadness,
And lifted me to light.
  Now I know
  I have no fear,
  For I am being watched
  By guardians above.
  The darkness
  Can no longer sadden me,
  For I am shrouded
  In my Savior's love.
Lord, You have
Saved me from sadness,
And lifted me to light.

February 2001

52

Awakening After a Close Call

Don't believe the Christmas trees!
Everything is so much more beautiful
And wonderful, and glorious
Than anything we can imagine
Or compare, or create.
Especially the Light, and the Angels!
The Light is so many things...
A window.
A tunnel.
A sunset at the edge
Of a polished pier.
And the Angels...
The Angels are more than
Just males and females with wings,
They glow with the Light
Of Every-color!
One color at a time,
Or all at once, or none at all.
But there is no darkness.
There is no darkness in Heaven.
And there is no death.
Even though we must die to enter,
As we face the Light and the Angels,
We are beyond any type of death.
Don't believe the Christmas trees!
Heaven is beyond human description.
Believe in the Spirit behind the trees.
Believe in the Life related to the decorations.
Believe in the Word leading us to our Future.
And always,
And always, and always,
Believe in the Light, and the Angels!

May 2001

53

Future Proceedings

Today,
I saw a
Funeral procession.
It made me
Think deeply,
About how
Terrible death is,
But how
Wonderful it is
To go to Heaven,
And see the
Face of God.

February 2000

Learning Love for the Future

Signal or Symbol?

Most people believe
"S.O.S." is a signal
That shouts
"Save Our Ship"
During times of distress.
Maybe people should
Believe it is a symbol
That prays
"Save Our Spirits" or
"Save Our Souls"
During times of distress.
Then, most people
Would believe.
And we could all be
Unified in an attempt
Towards the most important
Message of all...
"Save Our Salvation!"

January 2002

Inquisition

If faith is
Believing in something
Without proof
Because it inspires us
To a better life and future,
Why do we argue with others,
And even kill others,
Trying to persuade others
About whose faith is "right"?

November 2001

Seeds for Thought

The sword is heavy,
And piercing sharp.
Stronger than rock,
It yields a mighty blow
To the foe
With each assault.
The bow and arrow
Are light and swift.
Silent war implement,
It yields a surprise attack
To front or back,
From a distance.
And yet,
Stronger than the sword,
Swifter than the arrow,
Are words—
Among the most powerful
Of all weapons.
Words can tear and hurt
And cause pain and strife.
Words can heal and comfort
And sow peace in life.
Heed the wisdom, and
Use words with care.

January 2001

59

Dear Mr. Bush

You said we are caught
Between terrorism and hopelessness.
You said we cannot
Find peace in this situation.
I caught your words, but
I cannot agree with the conclusion.
Clearly,
We cannot perpetuate terrorism.
But perhaps,
If we choose to accept
Hopelessness with a catch,
We will find peace in all situations.
Hope, or lack of hope,
Is an attitude.
And an attitude is a choice.
In this great country,
We do have a choice.
And so, in conclusion,
We cannot get caught
With a bad attitude,
Or we are not choosing peace.

June 2002

60

We, the People

We cannot win
The war against terrorism
With bombs.
We must face
Such horror and hatred
With words.
We should not even view
The war against terrorism
As a battle.
It cannot be conquered.
We cannot be triumphant.
The war against terrorism
Is a real-life issue
That must be solved.

January 2002

Ascent

Let's take the
Bouldering mistakes of the past,
And the
Roadblocking challenges of the present,
And build them into
Stairs that support our climb into the future.

February 2002

Future for Life?

War and hatred.
Conflict and struggle.
Pain and strife.
Between countries.
Within countries.
Between groups.
Within groups.
Between individuals.
Within individuals.
Never past.
Always present.
Is there a future?
We know.
But we do not understand.
We realize.
But we do not learn from lessons.
We have wisdom.
But we do not work with universal effort
To change
What was,
What is,
What cannot continue to be,
If we hope
For peace,
For harmony,
For a future
...For life.

August 2000

63

Forgive to Forget

Always forgive,
But never forget.
If you forget,
When the lesson
Of the past is needed,
It may be lost.
But if you forgive,
When the lesson
Of the past is heeded,
It may be what is needed
So you can move
Forward in life.

June 2002

Micah's Lesson

Always
Forgive to forget,
But never
Forget to forgive.

June 2002

64

Peace Prescription

When we hurt another,
With our words,
With our actions,
Or even with our thoughts,
It causes a wound.
Some wounds are seen.
Some wounds are invisible.
Some wounds heal.
Some wounds leave a scar.
And some wounds,
Especially those that are
Inflicted or opened again
And again and again...
May never heal.
Let us take care then,
To not hurt another,
With our words,
With our actions,
Or even with our thoughts.
And let us take special care
In realizing and tending to
The wounds that already exist,
Or they could infect others,
And cause an epidemic.

January 2002

About Happiness

To me,
Happiness is traveling.
Not really "me" traveling,
But my Heartsongs traveling.
When the songs in my heart
Travel out and around the world
In the things that I say and
In the poems and stories that I write
And in the prayers that I feel to God,
And when the letters and words
Of those Heartsongs bring some
Peace to the countries and people
Who have war in their lives,
That is real happiness
To me.

June 1997

The Children's Psalm

Humble yourself like a child,
Through trust and forgiveness seek peace.
  Those who seek peace are truly
  The blessed children of God—
  Young and old in every nation,
  Joining in a celebration to Life.
Humble yourself like a child,
Through trust and forgiveness seek peace.
  The Lord calls the children
  In their innocence and gentleness—
  Patience and resilience He seeks,
  Faith and eager mercy they offer.
Humble yourself like a child,
Through trust and forgiveness seek peace.
  Unite in praise, share a song of hope,
  Our voices in harmony become One—
  The tapestry of creation, in a dust of pride,
  This shattered mosaic must be rebuilt.
Humble yourself like a child,
Through trust and forgiveness seek peace.
  Kindle the song in your heart,
  Share kind thoughts, words, and deeds—
  With all faith respecting The Message,
  All people will humbly find solace.
Humble yourself like a child,
Through trust and forgiveness seek peace.

April 2002

67

Timeless Existence

It is nice when people
Notice you are present, but
It is important when people
Notice you are absent.
It is said that "absence
Makes the heart grow fonder."
We should rather that "presence
Makes the heart grow fondest."
Then, even when we are
Gone into our future,
We still live in
The present of our past.

February 2002

Index

5/03

mL